Without a Prayer
Revelations of an Ex-Wife

BRANDY HADNOT

INTELLIGENT PUBLISHING

Columbia, MD
https://intelpub.com

Copyright © 2020 by Brandy Hadnot

All rights reserved. Manufactured in the United States of America. No part of this book may be reproduced in any written, electronic, recording, or photocopying form without written permission of the publisher, except by a reviewer, who may quote brief passages in a review. Published by Intelligent Publishing, P. O. Box 809, Columbia, MD 21044. https://intelpub.com.

ISBN: 978-1-7329425-8-5 (Paperback)
ISBN: 978-1-7329425-9-2 (E-Book)

Library of Congress Control Number: 2020900506

Cover Design: Brandy Hadnot, Intelligent Publishing
Interior Design: Intelligent Publishing
Editor: Lutrish Gundawa

First Printing 2020

DEDICATION

I dedicate this book to every person who feels as though they have failed at some point in their life causing them to become seekers of their true purpose, to the women who realized your true strength is not in your beauty but it's through the power of your prayer. It is also dedicated to the real superhero - the wife who discovered that a day without a prayer is not an option.

Contents

DEDICATION	5
ACKNOWLEDGMENTS	7
The Purpose	8
Little Girl Me	10
Search the Scriptures	13
I Should Have Waited on God	16
You're Stronger Later	23
I Once Was Lost But Now I'm Found	30
About the Author	65

ACKNOWLEDGEMENTS

I want to Thank God for Creating Me with a purpose and allowing me to go through the experiences that forced me to become a seeker of His will for my life.

The Purpose

    Everyone has a purpose. It's the reason we exist. It's our life's mission, the objective, the plan. All of this is wrapped up in one agenda; we were created by God to glorify Him. How this applies and transforms each of us is what makes it so special. Each of us has an already mapped out plan to follow, yet the plan is carried out at different times and at different levels in each of our lives. I believe we were all uniquely created. God took his time to form each of us and that leaves it all up to us as individuals to find our purpose in this life. It might takes both time and effort on our part for as we have all known and experienced, life can be both distracting and confusing. Only when we find our purpose and we start on our journey to do and be what we were created to be will we find our fulfillment. With fulfillment we will always also find

The Purpose

happiness. It is very important that we all know and understand that we are all here by design and not by accident. Even as young children when our purpose isn't known to man, if you would pay attention to them as they play and pretend, you may get a glimpse or clue of the designs of God. I believe that the plan for our lives has already been mapped out by God himself way before our lives actually began.

Little Girl Me

I'm reminded of the life of a young girl. This young girl played just as all young girls her age did. She received, as a gift, a Barbie collection. With this collection came a Barbie doll, some clothes, and - of course- dainty little Barbie shoes. The case opened up and could be turned into a house for Barbie. The little girl and her sister each the same collection. This collection would be taken everywhere the young girl went. Each day the young girl played with the Barbie collection with so much intensity of purpose and real intentionality of play. She became excited and very overjoyed as she rode home for she knew the fun that awaited her. At those times, all her imaginative powers would run wild. Just to stand and watch as she played with so much contentment one would see that she had disappeared into a whole new dimension.

Little Girl Me

The statement of 'playing Barbie' would be quite an understatement. She would dress her Barbie up in so many different pretty outfits; each one for a different event or occasion. She would comb Barbie's hair to suit the occasions. Her doll would be superbly dressed from head to toe. One day, though, the young girl felt something was missing. To anyone who had seen these young girls' growing collection, it seemed they had it all. The car, the house, the stunning wardrobe and much of the beauty. Each day as she played with serious intent, and with a very broad imagination, the girl then realized what was missing in her collection. Up until this point she was just as happy and content with just her Barbie. What her collection missed was a vital piece of the puzzle in the life of this young girl's Barbie. Her Barbie didn't have Ken. It was at that very moment that the young girl became eager to find her beautiful, elegant and uniquely made Barbie a mate. In the eyes and mind of this 9-year-old girl, she could do so much planning with Barbie if only she had her Ken. In her mind Ken would bring so much joy to Barbie. It was unquestionably her main goal at this time that as soon as her allowance was given to her, she was going to purchase Ken. The girl had already planned in her mind all the fun and adventure activities the two would have once her Barbie had Ken. Barbie was ready for the world. Of course, Ken was very handsome. Now this may sound strange, but Ken and Barbie got married. It seemed as though this imaginary child's play had taken on a life of its own. The girl once again saved her allowance to purchase a beautiful wedding gown that came with a long veil and accessories for Barbie. Ken looked dandy as he had on a black tuxedo. The girl's younger sister who was close in age by 1 year and who had her very own collection also joined in the imaginary wedding for her own collection. Not only did Barbie have beauty but the car the house, now she also had her Ken. It was the proverbial match made in Barbie heaven. After a few years had gone by the young girl wasn't so much of a little girl anymore. She was now a pre-teen. We can all relate to how it was at that age. The pressure to act a little more mature was on. What better way to show that you've grown up than to stop playing with dolls? So, the girl had a decision to make and the decision saddened her a little, but she so badly wanted to be seen as mature. One day the girl decided to pack away her large Barbie and Ken collection into her wooden trunk. Never once to be taken out and played with by the little girl again because surely all the other girls had already outgrown playing dolls by that age. How do I know so much about the details of this girl's imaginary play one may ask? If it hasn't become obvious let me say that I am that young girl. As you get into reading this book, you will see that my desire to be a wife doesn't change. As I imagine most if not all women who were once little girls have experienced. As I got older something inside of me began to change. This change is what I continuously ignored and supplemented by other distractions I allowed into my life. All the while trying to satisfy my desire. As you continue reading my revelations you will understand just what I mean. But I realized there's something greater at work because God always has a plan.

Search the Scriptures

It is at this time in my life that it has become clearer to me that having my steps ordered by God in everything I do in life is worth more and filled with more blessings than I would ever expect to receive.

See when God is ordering our steps, we know that we are in direct contact with God and he will be there to guide us every step of the way. We have no question that it is His hand in our life. The most amazing part of all of this is that even if we stumble and fall, he is right there to catch us. All we have to do is trust him and his word. The desire to have love and be happy, is very much still my desire. However, as life goes on, I have found that through seeking God for understanding and knowledge nothing could have come at a better time. I will recognize that Gods purpose for me has always been a part of the plan and whatever point God makes the Barbie and Ken picture real for me.

The sooner we fully understand and accept this, the closer to our true purpose in life we become. If we align ourselves with God's Will in our lives and seek him, then he said 'he will open up the windows of heaven and pour us out Blessings we would not have room to receive'. I don't know about anyone else, but I've come to the realization that I have delayed my own blessings and I decided to surrender my own will to God. My only regret is that this realization has come at this age in my life, but can be any better time than now? For with God time isn't a factor. I guess this is just some of the pressure that I once again put on myself.

Matthew 6:33
Seek first the Kingdom of God and All of His righteousness and all of these things shall be added to you.

My perspective on this all too familiar scripture is I know God is the source and anything we desire within our hearts we can obtain through seeking God and His Purpose for our lives.

Psalm 37:4
Delight yourself also in the Lord and He shall give you the desires of your heart.

Psalm 37:23
The steps of a good man are ordered by the Lord: and He delights in His way.

Deuteronomy 31:6
Be strong and of good courage, do not fear nor be afraid of them; for the Lord your God He is the one who goes with you. He will not leave you nor forsake you.

What has become my favorite scripture since growing into a closer relationship with God can be found in.

Proverbs 3: 5-6
Trust in the Lord with all thine heart and lean not to thine own understanding. In all thine ways acknowledge Him and He shall direct your paths.

I Should Have Waited on God

I Should Have Waited on God

Although I do have the background of a Christian up-bringing in the church, and I've heard ministers and Sunday school teachers teach and preach on the subject of marriage and how to include God in everything you do; you know how it is when young and vibrant. We think we know more than we really do. We hear knowledge in one ear but somehow, we find our own ways of understanding which are usually all the wrong ones. It goes in one ear and out the other. Well I was a typical example of this. Let me share with you how wanting what your heart desires most could come to pass but also how if your decision making doesn't include God and the plan that He has for your life it won't last long. I know we tend to make our own plans and have our own agendas in life, and we work very hard to make sure that things happen and go right. We let no one or nothing stop us from having what we want in this life. We tend to be inconsiderate as people. I know I can speak for many of us and if we are being honest, most of us don't even ask God what plans he has for us. What is it that he wants us to do, where is it that he wanted us to go, or perhaps it is simpler to just ask the Lord to show a sign. For those of us who do take the time to consult with God we probably don't wait for His answer. We are not patient enough to wait on Him we are quick to move forward on things that we ourselves may feel are right at the time or most beneficial decisions for us. After all this, we then wonder why our plans fail and don't work out the way we expected them to.

Isaiah 55 8-9
For my thoughts are not your thoughts, neither are your ways my ways declares the Lord. As the heavens are higher than the earth so are my ways higher than your ways and my thoughts than your thoughts.

So here I am I've finally reached the point in life where I've always seen myself at. I've gotten married and everything seems to be working out and falling into place -quite easily- might I add. He's working I'm continuing my schooling, things really were looking up, or where they really? Keep

I Should Have Waited on God

Reading and you will find out that the very thing that we are missing is the very thing we run from and which could be the very thing that puts us on our path to or rightful purpose. I will be the first to admit I am very much guilty for neglecting to fully understand just what the scripture in Isaiah says. I grew up hearing this scripture preached from and taught on. One would assume I know better especially being a P.K. short of preacher's kid. Honestly it's not until this time of my life that I truly am grasping Gods word through this scripture. Thinking back over my life, if I had only paused long enough to allow myself time and space to hear from God before jumping onto my next Lillie pad in life, maybe - just maybe - my purpose would have been realized sooner. At the very least I would be closer to it if only I would have allowed God to be the director of my path. A preacher once said during his sermon that our plan in life is already set. God's plan for each of our lives doesn't change. He's not making it up as we go. It's up to us how long it takes before we reach our destination in life. God is waiting on us but we are not waiting on God. This really resonated deep inside of me. Isaiah 55:8-9 came back to me again, God's ways are truly not our ways His thoughts are higher than ours as well. I am brought back to just a few years ago in my life. I really shudder as I wonder, I really thought I had it all figured out? This was the time in my life when I thought I was ready and prepared, and never understood or realized just how unprepared I really was within my own self. All I did know was I felt ready at the time. Never really taking into account that some things are easier said than done and you have to ask God to direct you and prepare you, and really wait for His direction and allow Him to prepare you. There are things we go through in life that are sorrowful for us simply because we didn't ask God for direction and we surely didn't wait on God.

Sometimes we pray for blessings that we ourselves can't even manage. Rather it's our insecurities, stress, anger, emotional problems or just our own selves. Either way we just are not ready for what we ask God for. Yet we are upset when we don't get to have what we think we need. A lot of times we may not realize it, but our own emotions get the best of us and cause us to miss our blessings. Procrastination, nervousness or simply the lack of believing in God and our own selves could cause our blessings to be missed.

We need to first be able to manage our own selves before bringing or allowing others to share our lives with us. All of this I can boldly admit that I am guilty of in my own life. If the older wiser and mature me could, I would ask the less trusting and impatient me, "are you ready". Knowing what I know now the answer would be "No, Not At All." Of course, I reflect on my youth days as well and I remember the countless lectures and conversations that I was blessed to receive from countless people in my life who wanted to see me succeed. These were people who had lived life and had the experiences to back it up. At the time I saw it as boring and couldn't see much of it applying to me because I knew I was different and would make better choices. So, I thought. I didn't know that being different never would exclude me from the trials of living life. Instead, it would most definitely make it that much stressful and harder when you don't understand that God truly has a plan for your life. I've learned, you have to slow down and listen to his directions. At times we find ourselves going around in circles, like a dog chasing its own tail. As I've previously mentioned, I believe everyone has a purpose in life that they were created to seek out and fulfill. Some people are blessed to find love and their purpose all at once. I strongly believe that it's never God's desire to have our purposes go unfulfilled. Yet the roads that lead to our purpose gets detoured in various ways. We all know that it's the enemy's mission to do so, however, sometimes it's our own doing that slows us down or throws us off track. For example, there are people who come into our lives to stay and there are some who come to teach us and help us grow. Believe it or not there are people who God allows to come into our lives just to be a door to our next level in life. I've experienced all of these at various points in my life, maybe you have too. If so, take a moment to reflect and see if you've experienced growth in any aspect of your life as result of it. If you have grown from it, you can count that as a blessing. Blessings come from different directions and in different forms. Yes, I'm sure there are lessons we may have learned along the way in the hardest of ways and there are some that were rather very painful and even sorrowful.

James 1:2-5

My brethren Count it all joy when you fall into various trials, knowing that the testing of your faith produces patience. But let patience have its perfect work, that you may be perfect and complete, lacking nothing. If any of you lacks wisdom, let him ask God who gives to all liberally and without reproach, and it will be given to him.

As related to my introductory story of the little girl that I was, the desire for family has always been with me. I know for some having to play the role of a wife isn't anywhere on your radar. You're content with your own space and living life to the fullest all by yourself. Well for me this has always been a desire since early on in my life. Like it was built into me and is naturally a part of my being. So after having gone through a few failed relationships early on in my adult life and having to learn from each of those relationships more of who I was becoming as an individual, I was brought to a point where I started to talk to God. At this point I was blatantly asking God to send me a husband. I was done with being introduced to different people because it never worked out for one reason or the other. They never seemed good enough and where full of either themselves or something else. Either way I was over it all and called myself relying on God to send me a man. I remember making a statement that This man will have to come knocking on my door before I accept another man in my life. I was done. But deep inside of me, I wasn't quite as done yet. A part of inner me still longed for a beautiful marriage someday. One thing that was true, I wasn't as fully prepared as I always thought. My feelings and views on marriage and the true meaning behind it has never changed. I've always felt that a husband and wife are the greatest asset to each other's lives. I believe if we are in the will of God and are aligned to His Word and His plan for our lives, we become closer to reaching our destiny or purpose in life. This is why we have to be certain and very careful who we attach ourselves to. Even a spouse could be the roadblock to seeing our way through. Being unequally yoked is how it's described in the bible. There's nothing more fulfilling as a married couple than to be one in Christ. We should be sure that the spouse we marry can also see the will of God for both of your lives. This can be very crucial to the marriage. Being in the will of God is where we will find our peace and joy and His blessings will overflow in our lives. This is what I strove to become once I began to pray for God to bless me with a husband. I knew that it was through being in God's will that my life would be blessed, and I was convinced he had a Man also waiting for my arrival in his life. My Christian roots ran deep. Shacking up with a man isn't looked upon kindly, especially coming from a household of being a preacher's kid. People seem to pay more attention to your lifestyle than most. Knowing all of this confirmed to me that marriage is truly what I desired. Looking back, there is so much that I wish I could change from the outcome of my previous marriage. For it's through my knowledge and understanding that I have gained the wisdom to accept and own up to my short comings as a wife. And that is what has inspired me to write my story. I want to share my experience with those who can relate and with those who are in the thick of it right now. I want you to know that it's only through my fight for understanding that I was forced to not only look at my own self but to also begin to find the starting point of my purpose. Which is why it's very crucial for each of us as individuals; as man or woman we need to know ourselves and know that God has a greater purpose for our lives. This greater purpose extends far beyond our relationships with each other. Of course, He wants us all to be successful in what we do; most importantly, He want us to trust in Him. So many of us are running from relationship to relationship and from one marriage to the next marriage seeking the answer to a spiritual question from a natural place and not even realizing it. We find it easier to deal with the flesh than to deal with the spiritual tug on our lives; which is why we are never satisfied regardless of where we are at or who we are with. It took me years of leaping from one Lillie pad to the next before finally getting to the point of surrender to God and His will for my life. Now I have a story to tell. I realize now that it was never about me and my will. I also realize God has to be in it for you to win it. He's our creator and we have to involve Him it whatever we do in life if we want to succeed and remain successful. Yes, this includes marriage. If we ask God for something it is always in our best interest that we wait for His answer. Even if we don't agree and don't like His answer to our question. Providing that we even think to ask. Remember God Knows best. A lot of times we ask God for things and His answer is no, or not yet, then we make the mistake of making it happen on our own and expect His blessings afterwards. God allows us to have free will, He allows us to live our lives and make decisions consequences of which even he knows we are not ready to deal with. Yet, for us those decisions seem to be right at the time for various reasons. The whole while we have left Him out of the equation. But God is a God of second chances. It's because of His Grace and Mercy for us that He remains with open arms to forgive us.

You're Stronger Later

You're Stronger Later

By the time you read my story I would have been divorced for close to 4 years. Within those four years particularly this last year I've done a lot of soul searching and have acquired a lot of knowledge through various ways and it's only through my unwillingness to give up no matter what life has brought me that I'm able to see clearer. I'm at this point in my life where I've become accepting of the lessons it has all taught me. I can own up to my mistakes and short-comings because I realize that knowledge really is power. The power isn't in who you're in a struggle with and who comes out on top; true power is in what you do once you come to the understanding of the purpose of your life. Then you will also understand why it's a struggle to reach that purpose. Imagine having to experience all this while trying to become someone whom you hadn't become fully equipped to become as yet. Simple reason for that misalignment being that you're not focused on Gods plan for your life. I started taking a deep look into my past and the different chapters of my life and tried to get a clear understanding of just how I ended up without the very thing that I had prayed and asked God to bless me with. I know I had been sincere and persistent in asking God to bless me with a husband and allow me to have a better life. What I should have been asking God for was to prepare me to become a wife and to position my life to line up with His Will for me first. However, my revelations would come later after all is over. I see now why sometimes God's answer is No, but we bypass the signs and keep straight on in our wrong lanes. We should all have a really good understanding that maturity in each of us is reached at different stages in life and wisdom comes by seeking knowledge. When we lack the important aspect of direction it's almost like driving blindfolded because we can't see what's ahead of us or even if we are headed in the right direction. I'm sure we all can look back and relate and say if I knew then even half of what I know now I would have arrived at my purpose sooner; or my life would be different; or I would have made a better choice. Personally, I would say I would have been better at the level I was at had I sought to find out who God created me to become. With that I would have found my power, my joy, my peace and I would have been whole. Then I would have been able to see my way along the path that He had already set for me. I can't put the blame all on my previous husband for our marital woes and why it failed. Instead I accept my share in the blame. No one who truly desires commitment and unity expects for it to end in separation or divorce. However, one thing that's for certain is if God isn't in it you can for sure count on failing in one area or another in your relationship. For some, it's most of the areas but we still hang on for various reasons of our own. You may be convinced or think that you have it all together and going smoothly but if God isn't in it, we may want to ask ourselves, exactly who is running operations. Some of our ways of operating as one are not exactly as one and we end up with out of the blue surprises when our foundation is shaken or when even a minor occurrence happens. This is coming from a woman who felt that she had the easiest marriage relationship I believed could ever exist. However, we really didn't know how to be as one and didn't have God at the forefront of our marriage. It wasn't because neither of us didn't believe in God. Yet it was the lack of knowledge and maturity within our own selves as individuals pertaining to God that caused our foundation not to stand as strongly as it should have been when we joined to become one. We were both going through the motions and imitating what we believed to be the correct way of handling things as a married couple. Every household, as we have been taught, has a head and the head of the household leads the house and makes the bottom-line decisions concerning the house. We may not have ever looked at it in this way, but a marriage is similar to how a business is run. Let's take a Corporation for example; there are key titles and each of these titles have an obligation to the benefit of the Corporation. Chief Financial Officer (CFO), who is responsible for managing the finances of an organization. Chief Operating Officer (COO) reports to the CEO and is usually in second command within the company and overseas the day to day administrative and operating functions of the business. Chief Executive Officer (CEO) is the highest-ranking person in the company who is ultimately responsible for making managerial decisions. Now to put this into perspective and see just how important God is to the marriage. A marriage set up correctly can run smoothly in its operations and be able to withstand most marriage crisis – But only if God is running it. The Father the Son and the Holy Spirit all work together as one. The CEO of Our marriage should be God.

We have to allow God to be at the head of our marriage and rely on Him to make the ultimate decisions and manage our marriage. We also need to trust that He will lead us to a more productive and growing relationship. That is exactly what a CEO does. We need a COO or Chief Operating Officer which we can refer to as the Holy Spirit. Having the Holy Spirit abide in our marriage gives us the benefit of being led in our daily lives, the Holy Spirit is our comforter and intercedes on our behalf and reports back to the CEO. When we are having marital problems we need an answer from God. Praying about our issues and allowing the Holy Spirit to lead us in the right direction rather than following our own advice - or anyone else's for that matter - keeps the business in order. Let's also agree that every company takes money to make money. Some also start up with the help of investors. To put this in perspective, the bible teaches us to allow God to be head of our finances. Having God as head of our finances and believing Him to provide for all of our needs, is the wisest and most important decision we can make. God is our investor as well. He invested in us through the shedding of His blood. Yes, He expects a return on His investment. Our return to Him should be our belief in Him and our relationship with Him. If we think about it most businesses are bought out or go out of business when the finances are mishandled as a result of not being managed correctly. Allowing God to be head of our finances will ensure that our wells will not run dry.

Philippians 4:19
And my God shall supply all your needs according to His riches in glory by Christ Jesus.

There shouldn't be any reason for us to be unsuccessful within our marriage with God as the head. If we set our marriage up to be led by God and allow Him to run it according to His plans, and His purpose for our lives we shall prosper in our marriages. This is not to say there won't be trying times throughout your marriage because, for those who have over the years managed to keep it together, I know of nothing but God as being the reason for your success and longevity. Although it is His desire for us to succeed, it's our job to put in the work to do so. We will get out of our marriage relationships the results of the effort that we put into it. Women when we need certain things from our husbands and he doesn't seem to understand, that's when we go to God in prayer and allow God to bring whatever it is to the attention of our husband. This is something that I failed to implement within my own marriage. I did bring my issues or concerns to the attention of my husband and expressed how I was feeling on the things that bothered me. I don't feel that he was equipped any more than I was to know just how to solve the issues maturely. What I do feel is that we were both trying to feel our way through the marriage and were never emotionally strong enough to deal with small issues that started to plague our marriage. Those small issues eventually became giants. I continued to express my concerns and how I felt that our lack of communication was the obstacle from us getting back on track despite the real issues that were fairly small compared to what was ahead. I knew that I was the more communicative one in the marriage, however, communication has to be two-sided. As women we look to our men to protect and defend us no matter what the circumstances may be. When something concerns one it should also concern the other to the point that a change takes place somewhere. Both spouses should then take the time to sit and discuss things. The most powerful language to speak sometimes is the language of silence and active listening. This is difficult to do when neither spouse will admit their mistakes and allow the other to express themselves without judgment or character assassination. I know you are reading this and trying to define the kind of marriage life you have. I will again declare; my marriage life was great. It was not any different from any other marriage but also just like most marriages our marriage suffered from lack of affective communication or should I say affective comprehension by both parties. The key word is affective because not all communication is considered as affective. When you're not yet mature enough within yourself - much less in your marriage to understand how different men and women really are when it comes to processing information. Affective communication doesn't exist. Thinking of what brought the two of you together in the first place and why you vowed to spend the rest of your life with that person and just how deep in love with the person you really are, should be a good enough reason to want to see your marriage succeed. What if it isn't enough? You may very well ask. I still remember the exact moment that I began to see my then husband in a different light. The more I found myself in a situation of having to stand up for the man I vowed to love and cherish until death do us part the less trust and respect I had towards him. He became less attractive to me and I began to feel the space between us continue to widen. I knew then that our marriage was failing. I began to think of all my previous relationships and why I chose to walk away from or just didn't care to hold on to. Maybe it was because I never saw a future in them. This feeling was very different, is was not just a relationship it was my marriage, which I cared about. We both became withdrawn from one another which really stopped the communication between us and made it difficult to try. This made matters even worst. By this time, we were at a stage of little to none quality feedback concerning our marital issues. A part of me wanted to remain upset however I knew this had to be resolved before we could move forward and remain happily married. Things between us continued to get distant as it seemed everywhere we turned the simplest of things ended in argument. After a while separation became a temporary solution. This wasn't the wisest decision to make. We both gave the enemy full access to come into our home and into our marriage and slowly pick it apart day by day.

Matthew 12:25
But Jesus knew their thoughts, said unto them:
Every Kingdom divided against itself is brought to
desolation and every city or house divided against
itself will not stand.

With us being as divided as we had become this was an easy task to accomplish. We had no unity and no true relationship with God as our defense to know that we were stronger in this battle together than we ever would be divided. We were too naïve as young adults to know just how important God was to our marital foundation. Had he been the head of our lives, marriage would have been solid enough that we would have gotten through the issues.

In the midst of the calamity the one thing that I didn't do was take all of these problems to God in prayer. I found myself alone and trying to fix this for the both of us. After being separated twice we had not resolved the same issues the first time and thinking things would automatically blow over. This was easy to accomplish because the foundation of our marriage wasn't as solid as it should have been from the beginning. We definitely didn't give God an opportunity to come into our marriage and work in the way that only he knows on our behalf. There was no unity with God in the marriage. This was my regret.

I Once Was Lost But Now I'm Found

I Once Was Lost But Now I'm Found

The position of being a wife is an amazing experience, very rewarding. The Most important thing a wife could do for her marriage is to keep it lifted up in prayer before God. Having a prayer life and a close relationship with God is very important. Staying prayerful becomes the glue that holds things together in our marriages when nothing seems to make sense anymore and the communication stops. When we lack the words to say to one another or we are tripping over our own ego, God is who we should go to when we need a mediator in our marriage. Putting the power of prayer over your family and primarily your husband is an unselfish and unconditional act of love towards him. An act that perhaps new and even some seasoned wives have yet to implement as a part of their daily lives. For some you probably don't think to pray at all until there's a need from God. We use God like an ATM hoping that our overdraft protection has kicked in to cover us without making a deposit. Praying for your husband who is supposed to be the leader in our household is so vital. Praying for him is not a means of gaining the control over him. Yet it is laying claim to the power in and of yourself and trusting God to transform both you and your husband as well as your circumstances within your marriage. In reflecting back on my previous marriage this is an area were my prayer life existed but not as it should have been. My prayer now is that God allows me another chance to get it right.

Proverbs 18:22
He who finds a wife finds a good thing and obtains favor from God.

The wife should bring comfort and peace into a man's life and the home. A sense of stability in a world that doesn't make sense. She speaks to his inner man or, as some put it, she speaks to the king inside of him. When he can't figure it out you both as a team with the help of God figure it together. She should be his best friend in a world where there's hardly anything best about any friend. She's the silent partner when he needs her to be. She should be the supporter of all of his visions and dreams even when they seem to make no sense. A wife is there no matter how hard or rough things get for them both she's usually the stronger of the two in more ways than one. The single and most important attribute that a wife should have isn't all in her looks or her or in her cooking or not even in her motherly potential. Her most important attribute should be her connection with God. Even when the husband isn't praying or able to get a prayer through there is just something about the prayers of a wife. Praying for your husband can be a sacrifice on your part as his wife. If I could change one thing about my previous marriage experience, I would for certain take time out and pay more attention to my prayer life with God. Even if my husband failed to do so himself, I now understand how important being a praying wife really is to the marriage. I'm not saying that I never prayed to God or prayed for the betterment of my marriage at the time. What I am saying is I didn't have a persistent prayer life. I was more like the ATM withdrawer and never made much of a deposit. Most of my prayers for my husband were as simple as Lord protect him and keep him safe. I reiterate we were a young couple trying to figure it out and mimic as best as we could the type of marriage both had seen our parents have. However, we left out the prayer life. I supposed we both just thought that once we were married, we had accomplished pleasing God and that's all that mattered. Everything else would work itself out. Boy were we mistakenly wrong! We forgot or never put much thought into just how much work we both would need to put into our marriage for it to work. Neither of us really put forth much effort into a true understanding of one another. Of course, I felt what every woman who has a husband should feel. I truly felt loved even though he was extremely quiet and a man of very few words. It all depended on the conversation as to how much conversation you would get out of him. I believe his love for me was shown in other ways and not verbally expressed as much as one would expect. As time went on during our marriage and issues came up one of the qualities that had attracted me to him in the beginning became irritating and the extremely quiet man of few words became less attractive to me. Although these negative feelings would come over a period of time, there came vital moments during our marriage when I needed the man I loved and vowed to grow old with to speak up and stand up not only for himself, but for his family. As certain situations transpired, I began to take notice of certain aspects of my husband that brought concern. These concerns would then cause me to become questioning of his authority to lead.

I Once Was Lost But Now I'm Found

This is where I really needed Gods help because I realize how wrong I was in allowing myself to feel this way. All of this could have been resolved if only I had consulted God to give us direction and strength to endure the rough patches of our marriage. If I could help a new wife in any area of her marriage as a result of what I've experienced, I would advise against coming into the marriage with a list of high expectations of the husband she wanted. I would remind her that he is only human after all. All things need to be done through prayer as a unit, never let communication between you get out of hand to the point that it causes your house to be divided. Always remember Matthew 12:25. If you're looking to get something from your husband that you have already asked him for, and he don't seem to listen go to God in prayer. Don't just pray to God for what you expect to receive from your husband at the time, but always keep your husband and your marriage lifted up in prayer before God our father. More importantly never loose respect for your husband.

Ephesians 5:33
Nevertheless let each one of you in particular so love his own wife as himself, and let the wife see that she respects her husband.

Without a Prayer - Revelations of an Ex-Wife

Although I don't feel the average person would marry someone if they truly don't love and care for that person. However, loving and caring for someone enough to respect them is entirely on a whole new level. What I learned through my trials of marriage is how very difficult it is to love a spouse if you don't trust them. It also makes it difficult to respect them as well. All of these work hand and hand. So, when one is missing from the marriage you can very well count on the other two to be nonexistent as well. Although it may not have started out that way somehow somewhere it happened. Some may very well agree with me when I state that I know the very moment that I started to lose trust. It seemed to happen gradually one after the other. After series of events took place that really were not that big of a deal to recover from. Ultimately, when the issues are not fixed, things build up and then steps in the resentfulness and bitterness. God's instructions are for each of us to; love his wife as he loves himself, and the wife must respect her husband. He's not saying we should fear one another but it's all about the love and respect for one another. I realize now just how important it is to give your husband who is the man you vowed to love and to cherish and who God blessed you to join with, the respect that he truly deserves. If you also notice the instructions given are different for both the husband and wife. It didn't say husband respect your wife or wife love your husband. Now why is that -one may very well ask. My guess is because they both work together sort of like if you are holding up your end and I'm holding my end up then we can make it together. Ladies, regardless of your negative feelings or quarrels with your husband always remember to respect him. I've heard it mentioned that a person leaves emotionally before they leave physically, and I am here to tell you this is so true. I could feel myself a piece at a time disconnect. Not only did I disconnect but I began to feel resentful and angry. Angry because I wanted things to be better and I wanted my marriage to work, yet I truly didn't believe my husband comprehended just what I needed from him. Instead of focusing on trying to make him understand and see just where I was coming from with my concerns, I should have been taking it all to God in prayer. Now I know and those reading will also know that if you need something to change or if your husband isn't giving you the answer your needing for whatever reason or for whatever issue you may have, remember God is always available to listen; take your matters concerning your husband and marriage to God in prayer. You may feel it's not fair or it's hard to pray for your husband especially when you're upset or feel wronged. Nevertheless, pray to God concerning the matter, don't ever feel that God doesn't want to hear from you or that he won't understand your need.

Matthew 6:6-8

But you, when you pray, go into your room, and when you have shut your door, pray to your father who is in the secret place: and your father who sees in secret will reward you openly and when you pray don't not use vain repetitions as the heathen do. For they think they will be heard for their many words. Therefore Do Not be like them for your father knows the things you have need of before you ask him.

Just remember to come to God with a humble spirit and be open and expecting to receive an answer. Set aside all of your anger, resentfulness and feelings of upset toward your husband and pray. God needs our heart to be correct so that our answers to our prayers are clear. There have been many times when I asked myself why I didn't take the initiative to lead the way for both of us to kneel down and pray to God together for our marriage and family as a whole .I'm sure we have all imagined and had ideas of how we see our family functioning together and praying together. Perhaps we also did vision our family gathering for prayer as led by our husband who is the leader of our household. Well this was my vision I felt that my husband should have taken the lead on that since he was the leader of the household. As a newly married couple then we started out praying together and somewhere together got lost. In a way I feel responsible for letting this important factor slip away from our marriage. I knew that when we pray and give God control, He promises to protect us and give us favor. Most importantly He promises to supply all of our needs. Still in knowing this I somehow let it get out of sight. The wife is said to be the glue that holds the family together.

    I had reached a point where I didn't feel I could any longer hold things together. Neither of us were prepared or even equipped to fight for our marriage. I surely had forgotten to pray to seek God and his council. I should have been more in tune with God and the directions on what He wanted me to do. I'm reminded of the scripture in the bible, Genesis 32: 22-31. Jacob refused to let go until he got a blessing from God. I should have been just as Jacob was. I should have been persistent and unwilling to give up. If only I was as prepared, then as I am now to fight. Yet it is because of my unpreparedness then that I have grown preparing now in ways that are all a part of Gods Plan. Some may even question how losing my marriage might be a part of Gods plan. My response would be a question thrown back at them on how we would know that it wasn't. Sometimes we jump the gun thinking that God is pointing us in a specific direction, when it could very well be our own will that we are submitting to and not His. God is said to be a God of free will, I believe he gives us time and space to make our own decisions in life. However, the most powerful decision is coming into the true knowledge and understanding of God and submitting to His true Will for our lives. The lessons and hardships leading up to this moment are what prepare us when we finally arrive at our submission of His purpose for us. Overtime my knowledge of just who God really is and how he speaks to us as His own has manifested many things in my life. Now I know just how to fight the enemy who seeks daily to destroy us in any way that he can. Remember the saying knowledge is power, it is through my seeking Gods word through the scriptures that has given me my power and has strengthened my spirit. I'm not in any way saying that I am perfect, however, even as I'm writing this book to share my understanding, there are things along the way that have made me grow both personally and spiritually. I have begun to see and recognize Gods plan for my life. As I look back over my life, I think wow! This is what God was trying to show me or this is why He took me through certain aspects of my life that I never understood until now. We all have gone through some things in our lives that we thought at the time very unfair and hurtful and for some a huge struggle to get passed. We may have gotten ourselves into some situations that we found hard to get out of and it took an act on God's part to get us out. We may have very well asked the question, "God why me?" the rebuttal for that question should be why not you. I've begun to recognize God's hand in my life over this small amount of time. There are experiences that have taken place that I know are from no other than the enemy himself. Let's just say that if it wasn't for my growth in God, I might have become shaken but I'm able to hold steadfast to Gods purpose and plan for my life now that I have begun to see it. For I know that If I didn't have anything worth robbing the enemy wouldn't be trying so hard to kill what I know to have been inside of me my entire life. I recognize myself fully now as a seed with purpose. One would put it as, as thief don't break into an empty house unless there's something of value in it.

Ephesians 6:11-18
Tell us to put on the whole armor of God, that ye may be able to stand the wiles of the devil. For we

Without a Prayer - Revelations of an Ex-Wife

wrestle not against flesh and blood but against principalities, against powers, against rulers of the darkness of this world, against spiritual wickedness in high places.

So, going forward, I've truly become stronger as I transition deeper into my newfound relationship with God. The thought of nothing being wasted is my reality. During my marriage I realize I never took into consideration a lot; being that we were both were young adults and didn't have much to offer one another when it came to talking through our marital issues. We were both stubborn and hesitant. I realized that we both put up defense walls as means of coping with what we didn't know how to handle. Through it all I've pressed to move forward and have thrived to get an understanding of where I went wrong as a wife. I no longer point the finger and blame my ex-husband. I realize it's my responsibility to learn from my own mistakes and become a better person for me so that I can be on my mission for my own purpose. I started by asking God to forgive me create in me a clean heart and renew a right spirit with in me. Psalm 51:10. To build me up in the areas where I once fell short, strengthen me where I was once weak. Give me the spirit of forgiveness and understanding. Allow me to make peace with what I cannot change. To also give me patience and a spirit of discernment. Allow me to Trust and to Love in spite of. Help me to understand that every day isn't going to be a day of honey mooning in my next relationship to purpose. Teach me how to submit and respect my husband. Bridle my tongue because not every battle is mine to fight. The bible describes the tongue as a two-edged sword, it cuts both ways. Which is why we have to be cautious of what comes from our mouths.

Proverbs 13:3
Whoever guards his mouth preserves his life, he who opens with his lips come to ruin.

Ephesians 4:29
Let no corrupting talk come out of your mouths, but only such as is good for building up as fits the occasion that it may give grace to those who hear.

Proverbs 15:4
Gentle words bring life and health; a deceitful tongue crushes the spirit.

Proverbs 16:24
Kind words are like honey sweet to the soul and healthy for the body.

Proverbs 18:4
A persons words can be life giving water; words of true wisdom are as refreshing as a bubbling brook.

Most importantly I asked God to teach me to become the woman, the wife that he designed me to be. To remove Brandy's will and allow me to fulfil His will for my life. Words have power -they either build up or tear down. I remember feeling so negative and full of strife over the things that I could not control pertaining to the lack of effort from my then husband. I didn't feel there was a balance from his entertainment life outside of the house. I wondered to myself why am I not getting through to this man. Why doesn't he see how detrimental things were becoming between us? How can I give respect to a man that I feel doesn't care about our marriage? I felt myself loving him less and less each day. Never once did I look in the mirror at my own self as well. I was very weak in my patience. Not fully knowing my own self as a woman made me fail to understand my position as a wife. I found myself focusing on age and time during my marriage when things really started going downhill for us. Being paranoid of wasting my time in a marriage that seemed unable to fulfill my expectations. Rather than understanding that people grow in different areas and on different levels in life and that it takes time and patience and a lot of work to build a great marriage. Great marriages don't just happen overnight or the next morning for that matter, it takes time and effort on both parties. At the time, I didn't understand the difference between the way women and men think or just how different our language of love or just our language in general really is. Submission was the biggest factor missing in the marriage. I'm sure some think that being submissive is a form of being controlled and not having an opinion about matters. I couldn't disagree more. Being a submissive wife creates peace and contentment within your marriage. You are serving your husband in a way that benefits you and your marriage as a whole. Ephesians 5:21-25 gives us the foundation of duties that are mutual between the husband and wife. Both are to work together towards the common goal in the marriage. Which is to be pleasing unto God. There isn't but one master and that's God and I feel the demise of most marriages come when we don't have this understanding as a whole.

Matthew 22:37
Jesus said unto him, thou shalt love the Lord thy God with all your heart and with all your soul, and with all your mind.

Pertaining to our daily lives, the husband is ordained to be the leader of the household under the leadership of God. This is where trust plays a huge role. We should be able to trust our husbands to make the wisest decisions when it comes to his family. To look even deeper we should first have the trust in God from the start of our relationship with our husbands that this is who he has given us to follow. Meaning we should always consult Gods approval before entering into a marriage. If we have Gods stamp of approval, then we know that God will see us through the hardest of times during our marriage. Both husband and wife should be submissive and loving in different areas of the marriage. For instance if it comes to the husband or wife doing something that would cause marital disruption and discontent once we realize that we are wrong , we should quickly rethink our decision and rectify the problem for the sake of peace and continued unity within the marriage. We should always choose peace over war. There are various scriptures that teach on the subject of submission. This next scripture really opened my eyes as well as convicting my spirit.

1 Peter 3:1-2

Likewise, wives be submissive to your own husbands, that even if some do not obey the word, they

I Once Was Lost But Now I'm Found

without a word maybe won without a word by the conduct of their wife when they see your respectful and pure conduct.

I'm sure there are others who could relate to this as well. We allow our actions to get in the way of things and this makes an already tense situation even worst. Simply because we have a lack of understanding of our roles as wives and husbands according to the scripture. Not knowing the rules of being able to submit has landed a lot of us in bad positions in our marriage. Everything should not be a battle that has to be fought between you and your spouse. The real battle should be in keeping the enemy from killing it. I now understand how important it is to have the spirit of discernment and how useful it becomes during the times when we don't understand. During the times when we don't understand our husband's actions or reasoning for doing certain things, wives, we can pray to God to reveal the answer to us. He will be sure to make it clear. A lot of things go unsaid and are not always communicated but if we have a spirit of discernment it will help us pick up on the uncommunicated words. We should have the heart of God towards our spouses. This allows us to see them in a different light through new eyes. The spirit of discernment also helps you to see the enemy from far off before he rears his ugly head and starts to meddle in your marriage. I did find myself questioning God. Yes, I know, we are taught to never question God to the point that we become upset. I can hear my grandmother saying "Baby don't you ever get so upset with God that it causes you to sin against Him, you get yourself in trouble that way, just talk to the Lord and ask Him , then you wait for His answer sometimes His answer is not what you want it to be. If He don't give you an answer right then then you just wait on Him some more. He hears you, but you got to wait on Him. He might not come when you want Him to come but I assure you He is always on time." Great words of wisdom might I add from a woman who has gone through the fire and the floods of many seasons and has succeeded through it all. I truly felt that by this time my husband had checked out of the marriage, or at least it felt that way. He was always so quiet, and you never knew what was going on in his mind. I felt as though he was leaving me to fight alone for it. Which in turn made me feel that he didn't value me or our marriage as I felt he should have. Well needless to say things finally fell apart. But they got worse before it fell apart. Praying to God then became the last thing I thought of doing when it should have been the very first thing I should have done. However, I wasn't there yet in my relationship with God at the time. I know that it's by God's grace that I am able to witness to you about it now. We as people seem to get ourselves into situations that become more than we can handle. But thank God for His grace and mercy. It's because of His Grace and Mercy that He still chooses to bless us when we mess up.

Lamentations 3: 22-23

Through the Lords mercies we are not consumed, Because His compassions fail not. They are new ever morning. Great is your Faithfulness.

To sum this up, Grace is God blessing us despite the fact that we do not deserve it Mercy is also not punishing us as our sins deserve. Mercy is deliverance from judgment Grace is extended kindness to the unworthy. After suffering from a failed marriage that looked so promising there was also collateral damage left behind. The type of collateral damage that if you don't stop to nurse your wounds from , you will forever bleed from the same wounds and each time you get injured the pulling back of the scalp would only make the pain and wound even more intense and deep. It just opens it up again. The type of collateral damage that only God can fix. I know firsthand that if we don't go back and nurse those wounds it will cause you to miss a whole lot of what God has for you in your lifetime. Regardless of how long it been and how we view them some of us are not healed from scars. In case you are wondering what type of wounds I am speaking of allow me to be clear. A lot of us are suffering from feelings of hurt from being brokenhearted, feeling lonely and lost after feeling as though you've been out of place for so long, that you feel worthless because you can't understand why you were never good enough. The feeling of being disregarded and stepped on and over because no one takes you seriously, feeling all alone because none seem to understand you, and don't care to take the time to. Here you are as a person trying to learn things working only with what you have to work with in life , not because you weren't raised and taught correctly , but because you never felt secure enough in yourself to want to get more information for fear of being judged or harshly looked at for it. So, you're all alone to an extent that it's hard to figure it out. You've cared for yourself for so long that you taught yourself to become self-reliant. Your family values are deeply rooted inside of you, so your family tradition and values are strong. You are wounded in an area of your life that if it doesn't get fixed there will be no peace within. So not only do you feel wounded, but you feel there's something else working inside of you. Ever since you could remember you've had this nudge in the pit of your stomach that has never gone away. So, you supplemented and filled the void thinking maybe if I can get on this level or that level in life maybe I will be accepted. So, you go through relationship after relationship searching for that one thing that could possibly satisfy your life and give you that satisfaction of feeling whole as a person, never seeking God long enough to get your direction. All you feel is a need for validation. Although your desire to be a wife and have a happy family has been your dream since you were a little girl you still have yet to find your own self. You figure maybe just maybe things will work out in your life if you could only accomplish this desire. At one point you give up hope. So, you talk to God and in being as sincere as you could be you request in prayer that he gives you your desire. Never mind the true fact that you're still working on your own self and trying to manage you first. So, you wouldn't know how to choose wisely when it comes to choosing a mate. Especially considering your track record of choices in the past. Your main focus is choosing someone who is different from the rest. One day you're introduced to a young man that seems to have all of what you at that time and stage in life have been searching for. He listens to you, he doesn't try to control you or the conversations, he's a hard worker, he's not a player. He also seems to be very interested in you and most importantly he passes the "Do you believe in God test". You know the one question you are taught to ask any one you meet before going further into getting to know one another just to see if they believe the same as you believe. Well this guy passed the test. So, you feel very confident and hopeful that you got it right this time because he seems very different from the others who failed. You think well I have been praying for God to give me the desire of my heart for a while now. Looking back in the past you've gone through the same type of relationships but with different faces. So, you feel like ok this time this is God's answer. Never giving much thought that you're the most communicative between the both of you and he's very timid and shy. Along with other factors that could affect your relationship somewhere or your future together. Both of you were just happy to have met, both had gone well through tragic situations of loss. Both of you needed one another in various ways that connected the two of you. Both sought validations. Both had a connection that was more of a need than a want. This is where we fall short. We all have been guilty of this at one point or the other in life, we've gotten into relationships that benefited us as being a met need. A need sometimes can be mistaken as a want, a need can be mistaken as a problem solver in our lives rather than genuine connection and desire to be committed to one another forever in God. This causes an unstable foundation and makes it hard to build upon; because what you now have are two people who rely on one another for needs that are not sustainable. It's easy to confuse what you feel as real and true Love and desire for a person that can cover your need with the real and true love brought together and covered by God. Just having someone there to fulfill a need never realizing that needs are temporary. As soon as the need is met whatever that need maybe things will become clearer sooner or later. I explain it as turning the lights on and pulling back the sheets. However what I mean is once we take a closer look at the reasoning behind it all , it could be for social status , passport stickers, or bank accounts, either way you look at it; if the love you are seeking isn't unconditional the foundation will crack and even crumble.

Matthew 7: 24-27

Therefore whoever hears the sayings of mine and does them, I will liken him to a wise man who built his house on the rock and the rain descended, the floods came and the winds blew and beat on the house and it did not fall, for it was founded on the rock. But everyone who hears these sayings of mine, and does not do them, will be like a foolish man who built his house on the sand. And the rain descended, the floods came, and the winds blew, and beat on that house, and it fell and great was the fall.

By simple definition the short answer for what is a rock as we know it in the physical form is that it's a metamorphic type of rock which has been changed by extreme heat and pressure. But by biblical terms and in the supernatural to all who truly believe, the bible reveals many names for God, including rock of ages.

Psalm 18: 2
The Lord is my rock and my fortress and my deliverer.

God is our rock for all who believe. He's the beginning and the end. If you build your relationships and marriages upon the rock, we can be assured that our foundation will be ever so strong. So, when the extreme pressures of life start to bear down on us causing our marriage relationships to go through the fire, the only change that will take place would be a change in whatever areas of our short comings. Rather, it be us praying to God Almighty to change the way we communicate in our relationships, the way we want to be loved, our finances, if we aren't getting enough attention Gods got you covered, or even the direction that we should be going in our marriage relationships. Whatever the situation may be God says;

1 Peter 5:7-8
Cast all of your cares upon him, for he cares for you. Be sober, be vigilant; because your adversary the devil walks about like a roaring lion, seeking whom he may devour.

Sure, I prayed to God for a husband in a way that I felt sincere with all that was within me. I truly felt that I was ready to take on the task of becoming a wife. I should have been asking him to prepare me instead. If we aren't prepared, we ourselves could cause our own foundation to be unstable, the enemy wouldn't have to do anything. I think back to the way I was feeling and thinking then and I realize all the while I was trying to fill a void that couldn't be met by any man. This void was deep inside of me and seemed to have always been there. Having the knowledge of God that I've grown into I understand it now.

Matthew 11: 28-30 comes to my mind.
Come to me, all who labor and are heavy laden, and I will give you rest. Take my yoke upon you and learn from Me, for I am gentle and lowly in heart, and you will find rest for your souls. For my yoke is easy and my burden is light.

God is a true man of his word.

Deuteronomy 31: 6 teaches us that God will never leave us nor forsake us. The bible also teaches us that God is a God of free will. He loves cares about us so much that He knows every strand of hair on our head at all times. Now being a stylist of hair, even I know that we shed a lot of those strands from our hair everyday. God knows all at all times. However, being a God of free will means God will allows us to make decisions in our lives that even he knows will cause us hurt and pain. Some decisions will lead us down paths that, if we are to be honest, we regret going down because we are embarrassed by them. It's been noted that the bible mentions over 65 times God having said the exact words "I am with you" and close to 400 verses telling the believers not to fear. This tells me that God has never left me and has always been there for me. I feel secure in saying that simply because when we ask God for certain things it's not always that his answer is yes. If we are, there are many times when we create atmospheres -so to speak, for certain things to happen, and we then become dismayed and upset wondering why did God allow such thing to happen. News flash! God gives us free will to make our own decisions. This doesn't mean He leaves us alone it simply means He's not in it until we invite Him into it.

Proverbs 16:3 says
Commit your works to the Lord and your thoughts will be established.

This means an inclusion of God in your plans, and He will lead and guide you. With Him leading and guiding you, you will never go wrong unless it's of your own doing. This doesn't mean the enemy will not come in and tempt you, but you will be strong and prepared to stand boldly in God and denounce the works of the devil. Bring it back to my own experience. We can't give what we don't have to give. Especially if we haven't truly found out who we really are as individuals. If we don't spend time with our own selves and get to know our own selves and Love our own selves, we cannot expect others -especially a significant other-to fill in the gap in trying to figure us out. Some of us once viewed things like I did at one point, the belief that perhaps when I get to this certain status or level that I will be a better me. Wrong. It's my belief now that it is our sole responsibility to become prepared for the things that we pray for God to bless us with. Many of us have prayed to God for things and that we say we are waiting for God to send or bless us with such as spouses, better finances, houses, better circumstances, or whatever your heart's desire may be. Then we never prepare by putting forth the effort to obtain these things and just expect God to do it. We are not allowing room for our blessings to come in because we are still cluttered from previous junk in our lives. Some of us are in relationships now and barely holding things together. If we paid attention and if we really had the direction from God to proceed right from the start, we would walk away from these now because we don't see Gods hand in it. Or it may be of God; but we are so set in our ways and too busy being just us that we don't have a clear understanding of what God is trying to do for us. I believe God allows us to get into our situations and allow certain things to happen as His way of growing us. Remember the saying; what doesn't kill you makes you stronger. Well that's where I am right now, my experience as a wife was short lived , however it has made me grow and has forced me into a state of self-realization. I believe this time God is preparing me and equipping me with knowledge and understanding that I didn't have before. All because I am seeking his wisdom unlike before when I desired the position but didn't understand my own mission and purpose in life. Which is another important thing to understand when we are in relationships; we may get the man or the woman that very well could be the right person for us, but if we don't figure out what our true purpose is, we will still be discontent. It is my belief that we should choose a mate that not only loves us unconditionally, but who understands their purpose in life as well. Someone who knows where they are going in life and it won't be just wherever the wind blows them. If they understand their purpose, they would know that you also have a purpose. Which allows for both of your positions to be manifested within your relationship. I will still state this has to be done by seeking Gods guidance. Which is where my relationship got it wrong right from the beginning. Neither of us were aware of it at the time because it was more built on need than want and position rather than purpose. This next scripture is one that really opened my eyes to see my way more and helped me understand myself and why things in life have always been off balance for me , it's helping me get on the right track of where I as an individual need to be before getting into another relationship . I am more equipped now to know who needs to be and who doesn't need to be in my life. This has helped me understand that this battle that I've been fighting started way before my existence as a person. All of the distractions in my life have been for a reason far greater than I could ever think of but I can hear God say, "How badly do you want it?" I really got excited once I began to get focused on what this scripture was saying, not just to me but all of us. This is powerful knowledge to have.

Jeremiah 1:5 says
Before I formed thee in the belly I knew thee; and before thou camest forth out of the womb I sanctified thee, and I ordained thee a prophet unto the nations.

This means we were all created with a purpose for a reason to fulfill a destiny set before us. Before we were flesh, we were first a soul. God knew us then, He knew our dignity, our individuality, our possibility, our legacy. He set us apart as His chosen ones. His love for us was there in the beginning before we were cells. We had a purpose even then.

Genesis 1: 26-27
Then God said *"Let us make man in our own Im-*

age according to our likeness; let them have dominion over the fish of the sea, over the birds of the air and over the cattle and over all the earth and over every creeping thing that creeps the earth.

Here is another of my favorite verses, verse 27 *So God created man in His own image: in the image of God He created him: male and female He created them. Surely this lets us know God created us with a purpose when He created us.* In knowing this we should know that God is not only our creator, but He is also our source. Making Him the head of our Lives because He truly knows all that we are going through and are headed for, all He asks from us is for us to include Him in our lives.

Romans 12:2
Do not be conformed to this world, but be transformed by the renewal of your mind, that by testing you may discern what is the will of God, what is good and acceptable and perfect.

2 Corinthians 10: 3-5
For though we walk in the flesh we do not war according to the flesh For the weapons of our warfare are not carnal but mighty in God for pulling down strongholds casting down arguments and every high thing that exalts itself against the knowledge of God

, bringing every thought into captivity to the obedience of Christ.

Romans 8: 5-8
For those living according to the flesh set their minds on the things of the flesh but those who live according to the spirit, things of the spirit. For to be carnally minded is death but to be spiritually minded is life and peace. So then those who are in the flesh cannot please God.

The enemy's plan was to incite Job to make a mockery of God and himself. He was certain that he could bring Job to his knees. Bringing all of these scriptures into perspective, for we know that from the beginning of time God knew us, He ordained us as prophets he created us knowing our worth. He knows us as individuals, so He knows our thoughts and our ways even before we do. He created us after himself so our legacy is far greater than we can ever imagine. He set us apart as His chosen ones. God created all of us for a purpose, I have no doubt about that. Now the enemy was there, and he too knows what was created in us. It's the enemy's desire to never allow us to reach our destiny. He knows if we reach our destiny we have won. His desire is to outdo God and try and prove to God that we are not Gods people because we are easily persuaded by the flesh to turn against God. So, if he could distract us long enough, we would lose our focus and our way, and never get to the promises of God. So, the enemy will use anything and anyone or he will get desperate and do the job himself, just to throw us off track. He will attack us in areas of our lives that he knows will impact us the greatest. Hoping that it would cause us to fail. We should take the servant Job in the bible as the greatest example. Satan knew that God had a hedge of protection over Job and he knew that he couldn't touch Job without Gods permission. So, he went boldly to God to get permission, which was granted –on condition that he would not kill Job who was God's humble servant. God allowed Satan to mess in any and every area of Job's life. His only goal was to see Job curse God. But even through all of the heartache and pain after losing his family finances, friends and everything he owned, Job never once cursed God. Satan was determined to prove to God that the reason Job was serving and so dedicated to God was because of all the blessings God has bestowed upon Job, he wanted to show Job that God wasn't who he said he was. For the sake of a point I'm making, I want to make mention that even Job's spouse played a role that is familiar in our lives today. The scripture says even Job's wife had given up hope and trust. She told Job he could as well go ahead and curse God. She reminded him of how God had allowed all of this to come upon him. If He indeed was an Almighty and powerful God, why would He allow this to happen to Job. Having lost their kids, their money, house and all else they'd lost. All that was left was curse God so Job would just lose his life too for there seemed no point in living. Job's own wife had given up on him. This tells us that her faith in God wasn't deeply rooted, as Job's was. In today's life we experience things in our marriage relationships that if we are not strong enough together as one in Christ for when the enemy comes in. He definitely will, because his sole desire is to destroy all that he can because he envy's us and the promises God has given us. We should be equally yoked and be strong enough to get through the worst of times together. This doesn't mean the trouble and problems won't be difficult or sometimes painful. What it means is that together standing in Christ the almighty, all-knowing and ever so merciful God, you both would be able to walk through the fire boldly together because you have God as your foundation. On him you can stand upon and you have the comforter which is the Holy Ghost to guide you through daily struggles. One thing we should be careful to do when selecting mates is to be equally yoked. Be sure that there's purpose for the unity. Or even if you're not married be sure that there is a common goal in the relationship beginning with God. It sounds crazy but even a spouse or a relationship could keep you from fulfilling your purpose. This is another reason having a spirit of discernment is so important to have on your side. With it you can see past the many blind spots that you normally wouldn't pay any attention to. We need to establish the true reason for having a person in our lives and be wise in who and how we choose a mate. When two people are together out of a need they tend to be codependent upon one another for various reasons. We then wonder where God is after things fall apart once we see that there's is no growth, and nothing seems to be right. There's still a void. This could very well be because we left God out of the relationship or didn't seek His guidance when seeking a mate.

Jeremiah 17: 5-8

Cursed is the man who trusts in man and makes his flesh his strength whose heart departs from the Lord. For he shall be like a shrub in the desert, and shall not see when good comes. But shall inhabit the porched places in the wilderness. In a land which is not inhabited. Blessed is the man who trusts in the Lord, and whose hope is the Lord. For he shall be like a tree planted by the waters, which spreads out its roots by the river And will not fear when Heat comes But its leaves will be green and will not be anxious in the year of drought Nor will cease from yielding Fruit.

Life is all about choices and we already know that God gives us free will to live our lives with or without Him. He's not forceful but His will is for us to walk in His purpose for our lives. We all have a role to play in life. Regardless of what that role or job is we don't have to be behind a pulpit or have a specific title to be a witness to God. I don't know how you feel knowing this but for me it has given me a new perspective and has aided tremendously in me getting myself prepared to receive the blessings I know God has been holding just for me. It wasn't until my writing began and reading Gods word, as I referenced throughout this book, that my own revelations became clearer to me. I've told you about my own life experience as a wife, and how my lack of knowledge and understanding not only of myself as a woman with purpose on my life but I couldn't truly understand my position as a wife to a man of little words and understanding of me as well. This adversely affected our entire marriage. I didn't understand just how powerful and vital praying for your spouse really is. It wasn't until now - years later- that I finally grasp it all. I guess better late than never, huh? Coming into a deeper knowledge of how God truly sees us really opened my mind and my eyes. I've shared with you how, even as a young child carrying over into my adult life, I've never felt that I fit in. At times not even among family and friends that I've had all of my life. There never seemed to be space for me to fully feel included. I've shared with you my desire as a kid playing with my Barbie collection and expressing even then my desire and how I seen myself through child's play. I've given insight on how I was raised and taught values as a young girl growing up. I've expressed how my growth as a woman has forced me to see the bigger picture of my life's journey and its worth. I see now that I am very valuable as a woman with purpose on her life. As a child of God more importantly I feel empowered. I can boldly say that I can feel God's hand in my life. He's orchestrating in a way that only He knows how to. I feel he's waiting patiently all of these years of my life for the moment that I finally grasp the bigger picture and understand just who He really is and how He sees me as His creation. What He has for my life is far greater than I could ever imagine. Even Job couldn't be broken badly enough to turn against God. His faith in God was strong that through all that he endured God remained as Job's God. As he held on. Some of us are like Job and some feel like we have been shut off from Gods blessings and that he doesn't hear us. We feel as though he doesn't see pain and the struggle we endure. We may even feel as though God has forsaken us. I can assure you that this is far from the truth. God cares for us and he's there and never left our side. He's waiting on us. Some of us aren't receiving because we are not giving. It's not a matter of God blessings us, it's a matter of us aligning with His word and His purpose for us and getting into His presence to receive our blessings. We have to trust Him at His word. Some of us have found ourselves going round in the same circle most of our lives. The only thing that has changed was the size of our circle and the tune. I want the readers of this book to take from it a few things. As women and men, we need to first have an understanding of who God is and what he truly wants from our lives. We need to find and get to know ourselves and love ourselves first before allowing our lives to intertwine with others who don't fit in our purpose. When we get to know who we really are and that we have purpose, the closer to the source we become. Our source is the creator, the creator is God. Once we get to know who God really is, we will find out that He's not looking for perfect people. He is not looking for you to be a perfect spouse. He's looking for those of us who know and can admit that we are not perfect but are working towards our purpose.   God wants to show the world just who He really is through us.

2 Corinthians 12: 9

And He said to me, "My Grace is sufficient for you, for my strength is made perfect in weakness". God is best when we are weak. His best work is done on a blank canvas. He can create in us a clean heart and renew in us a right spirit. He can make us as though we are perfect.

Revelation 3:20

Behold I stand at the door and knock. If anyone hears my voice and opens the door, I will come in to him and dine with him, and he with me.

God saying I'm right here I've never left and I'm never going to leave you. I will stand at the door of your heart; I will tug on your spirit. That feeling that you have had in your gut that's been nudging you that you can't seem to shake. That's me. Don't be afraid to let me in I will come in and create in your life brand new things you've never dreamed to have. I will restore your joy and your peace. I will restore unto you the years that the locust hath eaten, the cankerworm, and the caterpillar, and the palmer worm, has eaten.

He says I will repay you for all of your lost years. Joel 2:25 God wants us to be seekers of Him. It's through seeking Him that we find our purpose, it is through Him that the plan for our lives are made plain to us. When we line up with God we are on the right track in life. For those that feel that nudge and sense of urgency and unrest within yourself; that feeling of incompleteness -like no matter what you do you seem unsatisfied. It matters not what career field you're in and how many accomplishments you've achieved or how big your house and bank account are. Your life could appear to be great from the outside. You appear to be happy and content on the outside, but deep on the inside there's an unsettling stir. This is your true spirit, your soul, the real you that's battling against the flesh to complete the purpose for which God created it to have. To the women who can relate to having a desire to be married. I will say it's ok to have that desire, but you need to get an understanding and prepare yourself to become a wife. Never mind what the world views as a good wife or says you are.

Proverbs 18:22
He who finds a wife finds a good thing and obtains favor from the Lord.

I Once Was Lost But Now I'm Found

There are a few things you can do to prepare; these are tips that work for both men and women. These are things and areas within myself that I wish I had known prior to marriage. Remember knowledge is wisdom and with wisdom comes power to withstand the storms that are sure to come into our lives. It is our job to prepare ourselves to become the best person inside and out when we ask God to send us the person he has for us. We need to understand that God doesn't do things by accident but by purpose. In knowing this know also that God has to prepare that future spouse as well. One of my biggest hang-ups then was being patient and trusting Gods timing. All the times I thought I was wasting my time and life away not to mention not getting any younger, I never seen myself as being the one who was needing preparation. Ways that you can prepare yourself so that unlike me you don't go into your marriage with blindfold, which many of us do or have done. Many of us never see the full potential that God has created for us to be at, so we allow our insecurities, doubt and fear to trip us up. This is the enemy trying to make you feel doubtful and unworthy to have what God has already given us. If we rely on God's promises, we will defeat the enemy every time he rears his ugly head with the lies and negative thoughts. We need to know we are created in the likeness and the image of God; He made no mistakes in creating us. This is what the enemy hates because he too knows God is a God of perfection. God was pleased when He created us. I've never read in the bible where God rejected His creation of us. The word says Everything God created was good. If we lean and depend on God, He will always be there to fight our battles against the enemy which is a daily battle. The first act of unselfishness was demonstrated through Jesus Christ. God's only son Jesus took all of our sins and carried them on His shoulder. These where sins that had no belonging with Jesus at all. These were sins that He knew we were already subject to even before we ever committed them. We were so close to His heart even then, that He died for us so that we would have a right to live and breathe. So that we would be able to live and fulfill our purpose in life; to glorify God in everything we do. In life we have to become unselfish and take others into consideration. I think about it so many times, Jesus died for us over 2000 years ago. He put our needs and wants before His own. He didn't have to do it, but He did it anyway because He loved us dearly. He was preparing the way for us, then He set the bar high with an example of both an act of love and unselfishness. When we marry, we have to become unselfish. Some would argue that unselfishness would need to be shown from the other person before they themselves would consider being unselfish, some would also say they are looking for the perfect person worthy of being unselfish to prior to marriage. Some may also say a person has to have a certain status and look before ever considering them. I would disagree and say it is this type of thinking that will land you single for life or married but unhappy. An act of unselfishness and genuine unconditional love is the best gift to bring to the table. Looks and status are not all there is to a person. We have to understand that life is not and has never been all about us individually. It's about how well you treat others and how you feed into each other's life. Many problems occur as a result of someone being selfish. I learned later on after my marriage was over and after I began to look to God for answers and direction for my life just how selfish and inconsiderate, I really was being then. My lack of understanding not only of myself but of my position for being a wife and the responsibilities that came with it resulted in a lot of failure. Selfishness on my part came from a buildup of resentfulness and pain and anger when things became out of my own control and I didn't know what to do or who to turn to for sound advice. I seemed to only care about my own feelings, after not getting much feedback from my husband at the time. I realize and take into consideration now just how different men and women are. We internalize things different. In ways this works out for the better and in others not. I realize we should never allow ourselves to get so distracted and upset at our spouses that we lose the line of communication; it's not only in the need to communicate but we need to also comprehend what the other is saying. We are familiar with the saying everything should be 50/50 in a relationship. I disagree, both partners should come in prepared to give their all and the best that they have to offer. If each gives 100 percent and on the days the other doesn't have a 100 percent to give, the other still has 10 percent to give if the dedication is there. There should be enough unconditional love between the two to make it through. I am in no way saying subject yourself to be used and abused by this privilege. Think of it as a savings account. You set aside extra money in a savings account in case you need it someday. However, you can just keep taking from the account and never replenishing what you take. The account will then eventually be empty. Being able to admit we are wrong can be a challenge for a lot of us. Especially when you don't feel that you're at fault. Regardless of who is at fault neither person should be so full of pride that they can't admit when they are wrong. This leads unspoken problems to become big issues. Both people should be at peace with the resolved problem and be ready to move past it. If not, the problem could become bigger soon and manifest throughout various areas of the relationship. To the point that simple doesn't become so simple anymore and everything becomes a battle ground. If you feel wronged and disrespected or even left out, by all means speak up, otherwise we can't hold the other accountable for something they are not aware of. Remember we are all human and we as men and women don't always think alike in areas. God made us unique that way. Learn to apologize as soon as we learn of a problem even if the other person isn't aware. Pray for God's strength to help you admit when you are wrong. Bitterness creeps in when we are unaware. Now this next piece of advice hits right at my doorstep. One may think that I didn't take my marriage vows seriously or I didn't care. Certainly, I did take them seriously, as seriously as I knew how to at the time when I lacked the knowledge and understanding that I now have. Which is why marriage should only happen when both truly understand what it really means to be committed. If you're not committed to God first it's almost impossible to be committed to another person. Of course, between the two of us I was not only the oldest but the more experienced when it came to dating. By the time I became married I had kissed enough frogs and those relationships had their own expiration dates and were learning experiences for me. I was always the one to end those relationships for fear of being hurt more because while not knowing my worth I allowed myself to invest more of myself into those relationships than they were really worth. I strongly feel that because of the way I resolved my past relationships it played a role in my marriage as well. Not to say that neither I nor my husband tried because I want to believe we did. I will say, though, that I don't believe either of us knew how to fight for it. We didn't have enough encouragement and influence around us that we could confide and get sound advice without judgment. As I previously related, we didn't have God as our foundation to start with. If God had been there, I'm sure our marriage would still be intact. We didn't properly take our marriage to God and put things in His hands for Him to handle. I found myself giving up thinking this was the right thing to do when unhappy. Never giving God the chance to fight this battle on our behalf. Not knowing that I had the power if only I had the understanding and knowledge of who God was. Not knowing that a praying wife is a dangerous wife because she has a way of being in direct contact with God through the worst of times and He is right there waiting to hear her if she cried out to Him. Point is I never cried out because I didn't know how to at the time. Think of a baby when it cries. There are certain types of cries that come from a baby that's either a hunger cry, a pain cry, a diaper change cry or just an I-need-attention cry. These different cries are ways to get the attention of the mother. The mother then responds accordingly to the cry. Even as grown adults we have specific cries to God that get his attention. Once we have gotten His attention, He knows exactly what to do. Let me take this a step further and say God knows our problem even before we cry out to Him. He just wants us to cry to Him. Because if I cry out to Him this is effort on our part and God's word says if we make one step, He will make two. At the time I leaned on my own understanding instead of praying about it. Had I sought God's counsel and applied the principles that I know now to my marriage I would have been more than prepared to fight for something that I had prayed to God for long before I was ever ready to receive it. My story I am hoping should be a great example of both being careful of what you Pray for and learn to seek God for your purpose and finding yourself before intertwining your life with someone else who hasn't found their path in life as well. No one is perfect and we shouldn't expect them to be everyone travels a different path and our purpose is different, but we have to be sure that the person we meet understands the direction of their own lives and their purpose. I find it hard to lead if you don't have directions of your own to follow. We can't expect someone to give us something that they themselves don't have and this works both ways. Some of us are waiting on the other person to fix it for us which hardly ever works. If we want change, we have to be the one to make change. Stop putting burdens on people that they are not equipped to bear. I thank God for being a God of second chances. I acknowledge God as my creator and my source. I did something that I should have done a long time ago. I removed myself from interfering in God's business and His plan pertaining to my life. I've acknowledged to God that I know He has a purpose for my life. I gave Him free range to do with my life as He will. A lot of us find it hard to submit to things. At this point in my life I wish I had submitted before now. But now is just as good a time as any, because I understand God does things out of a sense of purpose and He's always right on time. I've asked Him to come in and restore me that I may fulfill my purpose. God's response wasn't slow. The answer actually left me reeling, it shocked me. He said I will give you another chance to get it right after you do what I told you to do. You're not going to get it back that easily, this time you're going to have to work for it. The same thing that broke you is what is going to fix you. It's for this reason that I trust God and thank Him for being God. The more I trust God and rely on Him the closer my relationship becomes with God. The process of writing my story is really what helped me heal and connect with what God has been trying to show and tell me. I feel His divine purpose for my life starting to manifest in areas that I've never experienced before. The revelations that came to me during my writing process is what inspired my Book Title. I became what many women unfortunately experienced before I could truly relate to those experiences. Being an ex-wife isn't the end of the world. I took my experience and I am learning from it. I'm preparing myself with the guidance of God to become even more of what I was before and never realizing it. Having wisdom and guidance from God is Powerful enough, but to understand that God has created you for a purpose and to pursue that purpose is nothing short of a threat to the enemy. Satan knows what God's strength is and to know that we are equipped to obtain it is threatening to him, his sole purpose is to distract and keep us from our purpose for as long as he can. He knows he can't stop us from getting to our purpose with God on our side, but he sure will continue to distract us and throw obstacles our way and attack us in all areas of weakness.

Psalm 119:105
Your word is a lamp unto my feet and a light to my path.

Many of you could still be trying to find your purpose. What if I told you that your purpose could be something that you're already doing, something that you already have knowledge of and are good at. Regardless of how big or small it may be. I believe it's our responsibility to find out. By truly seeking God I am willing to guarantee you will find your purpose. To the women who are married I will leave this with you. The very thing I feel I failed in my own marriage- Pray for your husbands. No matter how mad and upset you are at him. Any change that you may want to see in your marriage take it to God in prayer.

Ecclesiastes 3:14
I know that whatever God does, shall be forever Nothing can be added to it, And Nothing taken from it, God does it that men should fear before Him.

I Once Was Lost But Now I'm Found

Don't try changing your husband yourself do it through God in prayer. Don't have such high expectations for your husband, remember he is also human. When disappointment sets in try to look at the good qualities of your husband and remember just why you married him. It's the enemy's plan to set up a demise of marriages. More so, if you're not one in Christ, it makes it easy for him to come in. Luke 10:19 We are given power and authority over the enemy "Behold I give you authority to trample on the serpents and the scorpions, and over all the power of the enemy, and nothing shall by any means hurt you." Always pray over your husband's life. Through praying for your husband you will see him with new eyes. If you have God's heart, you are able to see things differently. Especially when it comes to understanding your husband. I love this next piece of understanding, when you pray to God to change your husband expect the change to occur in you instead. Change sometimes will come through you and not your husband. A praying wife is a strong woman, because she has God on her side, and she knows just how to access God's attention. Since women are naturally detailed, we are sure to cover all aspects of our marriage including our children. This is vital. Women just continue to be the praying partner that your marriage needs and don't give up come what may.

> 1 Thessalonians 5: 17
> *Pray without ceasing.*

> Matthew 18:18
> *Whatever you bind on earth will be bound in heaven whatever you lose on earth will be loosed in heaven.*

I don't know about you, but this too is very comforting in knowing, that all we have to do is use the authority already given to us by God to bind and release what we will in Jesus' name. This is not limited to certain aspects of life, yet it includes anything we need to bind and release. Most importantly to know that we serve a God with purpose for our lives, understanding that God has more in store than we could ever imagine. So why take the chance of not being in his will for our lives? Go after your purpose and be the best version of yourself that God meant for you to become. It is my prayer that someone has been helped and inspired to move in pursuit of their purpose. Just be assured that even when we mess up God is a God of second chances, and a God of completion. We all have a mission in life; it is up to us to find it and complete it. Through seeking Gods Knowledge and power, we gain the wisdom needed to find and

I Once Was Lost But Now I'm Found

complete our purpose. Just never give up.

1 Corinthians 2:9
"eyes have not seen nor ear heard, nor have entered into the heart of man the things which God has prepared for those who Love Him"

Jeremiah 31:17
There is Hope in your future says the Lord.

About the Author

About The Author

The Author previously released Book Titled Book Of Love "Him" available @amazon.com Barnes & Noble any major bookstore. Follow her on Instagram @ brandywineauthor Brandywinetheauthor@ fbk.com.

www.ingramcontent.com/pod-product-compliance
Lightning Source LLC
Chambersburg PA
CBHW071024080526
44587CB00015B/2489